7-04

Mozart

Other titles in the Inventors and Creators series include:

Alexander Graham Bell
Walt Disney
Thomas Edison
Albert Einstein
Henry Ford
Benjamin Franklin
Jim Henson
J.K. Rowling
Jonas Salk
Dr. Seuss
Steven Spielberg

Inventors and Creators

Mozart

P.M. Boekhoff and Stuart A. Kallen

KIDHAVEN
PRESS™

THOMSON

GALE

San Diego • Detroit • New York • San Francisco • Cleveland
New Haven, Conn. • Waterville, Maine • London • Munich

© 2004 by KidHaven Press. KidHaven Press is an imprint of The Gale Group, Inc., a division of Thomson Learning, Inc.

KidHaven™ and Thomson Learning™ are trademarks used herein under license.

For more information, contact
KidHaven Press
27500 Drake Rd.
Farmington Hills, MI 48331-3535
Or you can visit our Internet site at http://www.gale.com

LIBRARY OF CONGRESS CATALOGING-IN-PUBLICATION DATA

Boekhoff, P.M. (Patti Marlene), 1957–
  Mozart / by P.M. Boekhoff and Stuart A. Kallen.
    p. cm.—(Inventors and creators)
  Summary: Discusses the life of Wolfgang Amadeus Mozart, including his early childhood, flamboyant personality, travels, compositions, and musical legacy. Includes bibliographical references (p.   ) and index.
  ISBN 0-7377-1896-X (alk. paper)
  1. Mozart, Wolfgang Amadeus, 1756–1791—Juvenile literature. 2. Composers—Austria—Biography—Juvenile literature. [Mozart, Wolfgang Amadeus, 1756–1791. 2. Composers.] I. Kallen, Stuart A., 1955– II. Title. III. Series.
  ML3930 .M9B65 2004
  780' .92—dc21

                                                        2003009409

Printed in the United States of America

Contents

Introduction 6
   A Lifetime of Struggle

Chapter One 8
   The Child Wonder

Chapter Two 15
   The Young Composer

Chapter Three 23
   Seeking Success and Happiness

Chapter Four 32
   Operas and Funeral Music

Notes 42
Glossary 43
For Further Exploration 44
Index 45
Picture Credits 47
About the Authors 48

A Lifetime of Struggle

Wolfgang Mozart was born into a musical family in the little city-state of Salzburg, in present-day Austria. At that time Salzburg was one of the greatest musical cities in Europe. Wolfgang's father, Leopold Mozart, was a violinist, assistant **conductor**, author, and **composer** in the Salzburg court orchestra.

A Miracle Child

Leopold was married to Anna Maria, and they had seven children. Only two of their children survived infancy. One of them was the fourth child, a daughter named Maria Anna Walburga Ignatia, called Nannerl. The seventh and last child was a boy, born on January 27, 1756. Leopold believed that the child was a miracle because he was so small and weak it did not seem that he would survive. They called him Wolfgang but his sister called him Wolfi. His second name was Theophilus, meaning "loving God," but when he grew

Many people consider Wolfgang Amadeus Mozart's music to be the most beautiful ever composed.

older, Wolfgang preferred to use Amadeé, the French translation of his middle name.

Though he struggled his entire life, Wolfgang Amadeus Mozart is often thought of as the most perfect natural musician the world has ever known.

Chapter One

The Child Wonder

From the time Wolfgang Mozart was a tiny baby, he heard his father giving music lessons to Nannerl and other children. He also heard his father play the violin with other musicians who gathered at the Mozart house. Little Wolfgang listened and quickly learned, teaching himself to play the piano when he was only three years old. When Mozart tried to join in during his sister's piano lessons, Leopold decided to give his son piano lessons too. Wolfgang loved music and he practiced for many hours every day.

When Wolfgang was four Leopold gave him a small violin. Before he even had lessons, he wanted to play with the professional adult musicians who came to the house. He cried when his father said no, so Leopold let the little boy play along with them softly. Everyone was surprised at how well Wolfgang played, and Leopold knew that his young son had great natural talent.

It seemed easy for Wolfgang to play music because he had perfect pitch—the ability to name a note simply by hearing it. At the age of four he was even telling adult musicians that their violins were a quarter tone out of tune. The young boy also had incredibly sensitive ears, so much so that loud noises would make him physically ill.

Leopold hoped that his talented children could make his family rich by playing for kings, queens, and nobility in the royal courts of Europe. To prepare them for this task, Leopold worked very hard every day with Wolfgang and Nannerl teaching them to read, write, and play the music of great composers. Leopold's dream soon came true. By the time Wolfgang was five years old, he and Nannerl were playing concerts for the rich and powerful people in Salzburg and Bavaria.

Even though he was busy playing concerts, the young Mozart found time to compose incredibly complicated music. When he was only six years old, he wrote his first **concerto,** a piece of music with three parts, called movements, for an orchestra.

Musical Sensation

Wolfgang Mozart was a child **prodigy** and a musical star, playing to the most powerful emperors and em-

This painting depicts Mozart as a young boy. At the age of three, Mozart taught himself to play the piano.

presses in Europe. While performing on stage the young boy dressed as a prince in velvet and silk jackets with rich gold embroidery, a powdered wig, and a little gold sword at his side.

At these shows Wolfgang amused his audiences with musical tricks his father had taught him. He showed off his perfect pitch by playing complicated musical compositions after hearing them only once. He even played perfectly on a keyboard that was covered with a cloth. His amazing shows kept him in the news wherever he went.

Mozart's offstage antics also made news. When Wolfgang met Maria Theresa, the empress of the Holy Roman Empire, he shocked everyone, according to Leopold, when he "jumped on the Empress's lap, threw his arms around her neck, and kissed her good and thoroughly."[1] Then he amused her further by asking her six-year-old daughter, Marie Antoinette, the future queen of France, to marry him.

After the Mozart children made a sensation at home, rulers at other royal courts all wanted to see them perform. Leopold accepted as many offers as he could. He arranged for the children to play for emperors, queens, **archbishops**, princes, and other nobility throughout Europe.

Servants of Power

Although young Mozart was in great demand, it was considered normal at that time for royalty to treat great musicians and artists as servants. Little Wolfgang noticed that his father would often shrink in fear as he bowed and scraped before these powerful rulers to win their favor. Wolfgang was a very proud little boy, however, and felt ashamed to see his father cringe so meekly. This made him decide very early in life to never allow others to make him feel unworthy, no matter how powerful they were.

The audiences loved the performances, but many times, instead of getting money, the Mozarts were paid with gifts, such as clothing, watches, and other objects. This was no help when it came time for the traveling family to pay for carriages, inns, and food. Sometimes they even went hungry while entertaining the wealthy. At the splendid palace of Versailles in Paris, the hungry Mozarts were invited to a banquet but were only allowed to watch the royal family eat. Wolfgang was luckier than Nannerl that night, since the queen petted him and fed him tidbits from her plate.

The First Symphony

After five months of performing on the European continent, Leopold decided to take his children to London, England. At that time London was the biggest city in Europe, and one of the wealthiest. The children played for England's King George III and Queen Charlotte. The royal couple fell in love with Wolfgang and helped the Mozarts by paying them with cash instead of gifts.

In July 1764, however, Leopold became deathly ill for seven weeks and had to lie in a dark, quiet room.

At the age of nine, Mozart performed in London (pictured) for the king and queen of England.

During this time the nine-year-old Wolfgang composed his first **symphony** while Nannerl wrote the notes.

Going Home

Leopold recovered and the family continued to perform in different cities on their way home. But there were many epidemics in Europe, and illness followed them everywhere they went. Nannerl was sometimes extremely ill, and Wolfgang caught several diseases. In 1765 he almost died, and he was never completely healthy again.

Although Wolfgang worked very hard and endured long, hard journeys and terrible illnesses, his talents

Mozart as a boy appears at a royal wedding. Even as a child, Mozart was famous throughout Europe.

made him happy. Everywhere he went young Mozart listened to different musical styles. He met every important musician of his time and heard every kind of music being played.

With his ears tuned to perfect pitch, he seemed to remember everything he heard. And everywhere he went Wolfgang composed new pieces inspired by the different kinds of music he heard. His hands and his feet seemed to be always in motion, as if he were listening to music in his mind and playing it on an imaginary piano. Finally, after three long years giving concerts all over Europe, the Mozarts decided to return to Salzburg. Although he was only ten, Wolfgang was a musical superstar known throughout Europe.

Chapter Two

The Young Composer

Although the Mozarts returned home to Salzburg, Leopold wanted to continue making money by touring with his children. In 1767 the family set out for Vienna, but Wolfgang and Nannerl became ill once again, this time with smallpox. Their concerts were canceled and many Europeans worried that the talented children might die. After many weeks lying in a darkened room, the children recovered. But for the rest of his life, Wolfgang's face was scarred with pockmarks from the disease.

As he grew older Mozart developed a keen interest in writing **operas**. These complicated pieces are theatrical works in which humorous or dramatic stories, usually written by an author or poet called a librettist, are set to music. Mozart's first opera, *The Pretend Idiot*, written when he was only eleven, was not well received. Hoping his son would learn more about the musical form, Leopold took Wolfgang on a tour of Italy where opera was the most popular style of music.

In Milan Mozart spent hours at the opera house listening to composers talk, watching conductors, and

The Mozart family, shown in this portrait, performed music for audiences in cities across Europe.

making friends with the singers. There, a nobleman who befriended the Mozarts asked Wolfgang to compose an opera of his own.

A Teenage Talent

After leaving Milan young Mozart continued to play concerts to enchanted audiences throughout Europe. Even during this busy time, however, Wolfgang composed music on the road every day until his fingers ached. Finally the opera, called *Mithridate, King of Pontus,* was performed at the Milan Opera House in December 1770. In addition to writing the opera, the fourteen-year-old Mozart was **director** of the work, that is, he led the orchestra and instructed the singers and actors. The curiosity over a teenager composing and directing an opera led to great public interest, and when *Mithridate* was performed, it was a huge success.

Mozart was soon asked to write the music for another opera, *Ascanio in Alba*. But when it opened in October 1771, it was more popular than another opera written by the empress's favorite composer. This made her angry and she advised other royalty not to hire Mozart.

Return to Salzburg

The Mozarts visited Italy two more times in the following three years, looking for a permanent job at one of the royal courts for Wolfgang. Although his performances and operas were well liked, his requests for work were repeatedly refused. There was a bright side to this period, however. During his travels Mozart met many Italian musicians and learned their styles of music. Inspired by his growing knowledge, Mozart composed constantly. By 1773 he had written more than twenty symphonies, several **string quartets**, and three short operas, in addition to several compositions used for religious services.

Although he continued to grow as a musician, Mozart was forced to deal with the fact that he was no longer a child prodigy. Since he had become a teenager, royalty were not as interested in his talents. In addition, he was not as attractive as he was when he was a small child. In fact, his pockmarked skin was a yellowish color and his head, full of bushy fair hair, was too big for his small body. His nose was long, his chin short, and his blue eyes—which bulged out of his head—could not see very far.

Though he was no longer cute and adorable, young Wolfgang was one of the most amazing musicians in Europe. But he could not find a rich person to support his work. Reluctantly the Mozarts returned to Salzburg in 1773 when Wolfgang was seventeen.

A Job in Salzburg

The next few years in Salzburg were dull and miserable compared with the excitement of touring the royal courts of Europe. Mozart was able to find work, however, as a concert director and court organist for Archbishop Hieronymus von Colloredo.

The archbishop was a strict and unpopular ruler who ordered Mozart to write simple music for church services, often at the last minute. He also treated Mozart badly, paid him poorly, and had

As a teenager in Sazlburg, Mozart found work as the concert director at the court of the archbishop.

little appreciation for his amazing talents or his brilliant ideas.

To add to Mozart's problems, the archbishop would not allow him to travel for fear he would find work elsewhere. Despite this ban Mozart sneaked away to Vienna where he met Joseph Haydn, the most important and successful composer in Europe. The two young composers quickly became friends. Mozart was able to learn a great deal from Haydn who had just published a very exciting and original set of string quartets.

Back in Salzburg Mozart wrote dozens of pieces of music of all kinds, all without recognition for his talent and his hard work. Despite his father's advice Mozart refused to court the aristocrats or write the kind of popular music that pleased them. Instead he spent his time in taverns and coffeehouses with other musicians.

Composing

In 1774, when he was eighteen years old, Mozart was finally given a chance to show his talents once again when the elector of Bavaria asked him write an opera for the Munich carnival. When it opened, Mozart's comic opera, *The Pretend Gardener Girl* was a major success. Mozart wrote to Leopold about his triumph:

My opera was put on yesterday . . . and turned out so well that I cannot possibly describe to Mama the storms of applause. In the first place

This illustration shows a court reception held for Mozart. The composer attended many such parties held in his honor.

the whole theater was so jammed full that many people had to be turned away. After every aria there was a regular thunder of clapping and shouts of *Viva maestro.* . . . When the opera was over, during the time when the audience is usually quiet until the ballet begins, we heard nothing but clapping and shouts of "Bravo."[2]

With his newfound popularity Mozart attended many parties and was treated like a star. He was high-spirited, very intelligent, and quite excited, and at these gatherings the composer made himself the center of attention. Deep down, however, Mozart was very insecure and craved encouragement, praise, support, and sympathy.

This popular support made it even harder when the composer had to go back to his boring job in Salzburg. While he was at work, however, he had many hours to explore different ways of writing music. Mozart soon found that he could compose any kind of music, including symphonies, serenades, violin concertos, and piano concertos. He was the first to compose piano

Mozart composed music for many different instruments, including pieces for the harpsichord (pictured).

concertos as they are known today—as long, moody, musical exchanges between the orchestra and piano.

Mozart's newest music was widely celebrated in Salzburg, even by the archbishop who finally realized that he had a genius working for him. At the age of twenty-one, however, Mozart decided he would once again journey to Paris to seek a patron. Leopold could not travel because he did not want to lose his job with the archbishop. For the first time in his life, Mozart would travel far from his father and try to find success on his own.

Chapter Three

Seeking Success and Happiness

Although Mozart was going to Paris without his father in 1777, Leopold refused to give up control of his son's life. Since he could not leave his job, he sent his wife, Anna Maria, with Mozart to make sure he acted respectfully to others and looked for work. Anna Maria was also instructed to write Leopold every day to tell him everything that happened with their son.

At the age of twenty-one, Mozart traveled to Paris looking for a wealthy aristocrat to support him as a musician.

In Paris Wolfgang spent a lot of money riding around in cold, damp, rented carriages visiting royalty and aristocrats who might become patrons. But Mozart's clothing was not fancy enough to impress the wealthy nobles, and the composer thought they acted snobbish and unfeeling toward him. In turn, the royalty thought Mozart was a rude, conceited show-off. Because he believed so strongly in his own talent, young Mozart made enemies much more easily than he made friends. He would not treat rulers with as much respect as they demanded.

Learning the Hard Way

When playing with court musicians, Mozart often scorned them and sarcastically pointed out the lack of daring and imagination in their music. Because of Mozart's sensitivity to sound, much of what was acceptable music to others was boring or even physically painful to him. The almost impossibly delicate balance of instruments in his music required very skilled, sensitive, sympathetic musicians to play it, and a very special kind of patron to pay them.

Although he composed beautiful music in Paris, other musicians sometimes worked against him. For example, the sheet music to one of his compositions disappeared before it was performed. He expressed his feelings about this in a letter to his father: "If there were a place where people had ears, hearts to feel with, and even a spark of understanding of music and taste, I would laugh heartily at such things. But I dwell among idiots and beasts (as far as music is concerned)."[3]

Going Home Again

Mozart wanted a patron with the imagination and sympathy to let him take advantage of the marvelous ideas that constantly rushed through his head. But he hated to beg for appointments from assistants and secretaries who treated him with contempt.

Mozart's efforts in Paris had turned to failure. Then, on July 3, 1778, tragedy struck when Anna Maria died suddenly. Wolfgang was completely alone

After the sudden death of Mozart's mother in Paris, the composer returned to his job with the archbishop of Salzburg.

for the first time in his life and full of grief over her loss. Depressed, desperate, and disappointed, Mozart returned to Salzburg just before his twenty-third birthday. In spite of his hurt feelings, he never doubted his talent. He wrote to his father and said: "If the Archbishop would trust me, I should soon make his orchestra famous: of this there is no doubt."[4] The archbishop gave him the job he wanted as court organist, as well as more money and more freedom to come and go as he wished.

When Mozart visited Vienna, the archbishop forced him to lodge in the servant quarters of this house.

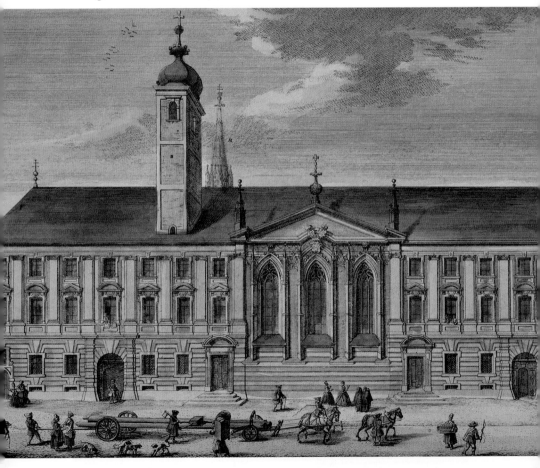

Star or Servant?

What Mozart wanted more than anything else was to write music for operas. Finally, in 1780, friends in Munich got him a job writing a serious opera called *Idomeneo, King of Crete* for the Munich carnival of 1781. Although Mozart thought the ancient story was not very exciting, he brought it to life with daring, dramatic, and lively music. Audiences cheered the emotional music that inspired feelings of joy, sorrow, rage, and grief.

Critics noted that Mozart's music, which had always been graceful, melodious, and clear, was becoming deep, magnificent, imaginative, and striking in its greatness. And the opera was a breakthrough for the composer. After hearing it, several noblemen who openly admired Mozart's great talent, befriended him and made him feel like a star again.

Mozart was enjoying huge success in Munich when he was ordered by the archbishop to join the other musicians in Vienna at once for the crowning of the new emperor, Joseph II. When Mozart arrived in Vienna, the archbishop made him live and eat with the servants and would not let him make money giving his own concerts. Mozart felt frustrated and began to treat the archbishop rudely.

Courageous Changes

Mozart's relationship with the archbishop had never been good. The archbishop insulted him and humiliated him constantly. The two had a terrible, loud argument, and Mozart called the archbishop the "archbooby." As Mozart was going out the door to leave for good, the archbishop's assistant gave him a swift kick in the rear.

After this final humiliation Mozart went to live in Vienna with the Webers, a family of musicians. He

After leaving the archbishop, Mozart lived with the Weber family in the house on the left.

had no money and he begged his father to stop hurting his self-respect by writing harsh, critical letters. On December 15, 1781, he wrote a long letter to his father saying that he planned to marry Constanze Weber.

Mozart's father was very upset, because her musical family did not have the money or the reputation to help his son's career. He wrote letters to Wolfgang telling him that it would be a huge mistake to marry Constanze. Wolfgang and Constanze were married anyway at St. Stephen's Cathedral in August 1782. His father never forgave him and never accepted Constanze as a daughter-in-law.

Sympathy and Imagination

Although he did not have a job, Mozart found a number of patrons to support his music. He worked as a freelance musician, giving concerts and music lessons and composing. He set up concerts to perform his new compositions and sold tickets to his friends and admirers. And he wrote the music for a successful comic opera called *The Abduction from the Harem*. Characters in the opera included servants who were the equals of the masters, one of Mozart's favorite themes.

Finally Mozart was completely on his own, the servant of no one, and his music became deeper and more confident, powerful, and brilliant. Everything he touched became a masterpiece. His deep, passionate music demanded sympathy and imagination in his listeners, however, and not everyone liked it. Some people thought it was too complicated, lavish, and grand.

Fortunately Mozart's marriage was full of sympathy and imagination. Constanze was lively and fun like her husband. But her health was very delicate, and Mozart often had to send her to expensive spas to recover. In June 1783 their first child was born. A few weeks later they left the baby with a nurse and went to stay in Salzburg with Leopold and Nannerl for three months. It was a very difficult time. Mozart's father and sister did not approve of Constanze. Worse yet, the baby died while they were away. Shaken with grief, guilt, and anger towards his family, this was the last time Mozart ever went to back to his hometown.

Finding Happiness

Back in Vienna Mozart set aside his sadness and composed amazing new works. His performances often drew large crowds and he remained very popular. As a

In Vienna Mozart composed some of his finest music.

star the composer attended many parties and often stayed out late with his friends. This lifestyle was not healthy, however, and in 1784 Mozart fell seriously ill with a kidney infection. But he was soon cheered by the birth of his son, Carl Thomas, one of only two of the six Mozart children who survived.

At the age of twenty-eight Mozart was finally finding happiness. Although he had been an entertainer for twenty-four years, his life was often wracked by sickness, depression, and grief. Through his tears he continued to write amazing compositions that brought joy to thousands of people. And although he had written some of the best music the world had ever known, his greatest inspirations lay in the year ahead.

Operas and Funeral Music

Mozart had been wanting to write the world's greatest opera since he was only eleven years old. He found it very difficult, however, to find a good story—called a **libretto**—that he felt was worthy of his musical talents. After rejecting more than a hundred librettos, Mozart met Lorenzo da Ponte, a poet and librettist who was a musical director for the emperor in Vienna. The two men found that they had an incredible creative chemistry and quickly created three unforgettable operas between 1786 and 1790. As usual not everyone loved Mozart's work.

The first opera, *The Marriage of Figaro*, was based on a play in which the servants were portrayed as clever and able to rebel against their rulers. The play had been banned in Austria because the emperor thought it might inspire a revolution. Da Ponte, however, convinced the emperor to let them perform the opera with the most rebellious parts taken out.

The Marriage of Figaro was funny and realistic, and some of the tunes became instantly popular. But the show was not very successful in Vienna where powerful court musicians, at the emperor's orders, played their parts with little enthusiasm.

Prague

Life improved for Mozart in 1787 when he took *The Marriage of Figaro* to Prague, in what is now the Czech Republic. Here the opera was an enormous success, and people treated Mozart like a modern-day rock star. During rehearsals the musicians performed with enthusiasm, delighting the composer. One of the singers, Michael Kelly, recalled that Mozart's face "lighted up with the glowing rays of genius;—it is impossible to describe it, as it would be to paint sunbeams."[5]

The music was embraced by musicians all over the city, and people began singing and dancing to the catchy tunes at fancy balls, in taverns, and in dance halls. Mozart wrote to a friend, "I looked on . . . with the greatest pleasure while all these people flew about in sheer delight to the music of my *Figaro*. . . . For here they talk about nothing but *Figaro*. No opera is drawing like *Figaro*. Nothing, nothing but *Figaro*. Certainly a great honor for me."[6] Mozart enjoyed this honor so much he was inspired to write a new symphony called *Prague*.

Mozart also wrote a comic opera in Prague, *Don Giovanni*, that has remained popular for centuries. Like *Figaro*, *Don Giovanni* was a great hit in Prague, and Mozart felt happy and secure, possibly for the first time since he was a child.

Young Mozart
At the age of four Mozart was given his first instrument, a violin, and began playing music.

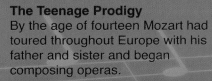

The Teenage Prodigy
By the age of fourteen Mozart had toured throughout Europe with his father and sister and began composing operas.

Rich and Poor

After his successful journey Mozart returned to Vienna in 1787, and the emperor gave him a job composing dances for the annual ball. Although he was paid well for a small amount of work, it was not enough money for Mozart's expensive food, drink, clothing, and hair care. "Too much for what I do, too little for what I could do,"[7] Mozart complained. Without one good patron to support all of his projects, Mozart became one of history's first freelance musicians.

During this period Mozart was often able to play sold-out concerts and earn a lot of money. In spite of his success as a musician, he was in constant financial trouble. He spent more money than he earned, lived in costly apartments, and gave freely to his friends. He

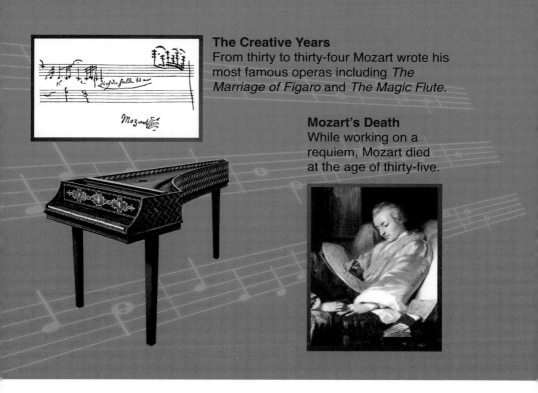

The Creative Years
From thirty to thirty-four Mozart wrote his most famous operas including *The Marriage of Figaro* and *The Magic Flute.*

Mozart's Death
While working on a requiem, Mozart died at the age of thirty-five.

was continually changing residences. He lived in eleven different apartments over the course of nine years, often moving when he could not pay the rent.

Fortunately Mozart had wealthy friends who were willing to loan him money. By June 1788 he was writing letters to them almost every day begging for money. He and Constanze moved to a cheaper suburb, where one of their babies died. During this period of grief, Mozart wrote his three last and finest symphonies in a matter of only a few weeks.

New Relationship, New Opera

In 1789 Mozart and da Ponte wrote another opera called *They're All the Same.* Although the opera was more popular than the two before it, the emperor died soon after the first performance. All the theaters in Vienna were shut down while the court mourned his death. The new emperor, Leopold II, was not interested in music, and da Ponte lost his job and left Vienna.

In 1791 Mozart worked with a new librettist, actor Emanuel Schikaneder, to create a fairy-tale opera called *The Magic Flute*. Schikaneder owned a big theater in the suburbs, and Mozart composed the magical comic opera for his middle-class audience. In that happy time in July, his second surviving child, Franz Xavier, was born.

The Beginning of the End

Meanwhile a mysterious stranger arrived. He offered Mozart a good price to write a piece of funeral music called a requiem mass. Mozart was told to tell no one that he was composing it. The stranger would not tell Mozart who he was or who the music was for. Badly in need of money, Mozart accepted this strange job.

At the same time the new emperor asked Mozart to write a serious opera, *The Clemency of Titus*, to be performed very soon at his crowning ceremony in Prague. Although Mozart was busy with the requiem mass and *The Magic Flute*, he could not turn down a request from the emperor.

Desperate to complete the work, Mozart wrote *The Clemency of Titus* during an eighteen-day carriage journey to Prague. But during his stay in Prague he got sick and was forced to take medicine every day. When the opera was finally performed on September 6, one of the royal ladies called it a beastly bore.

Don Jaun is pictured in a scene from *Don Giovanni,* a comic opera Mozart wrote while in Prague.

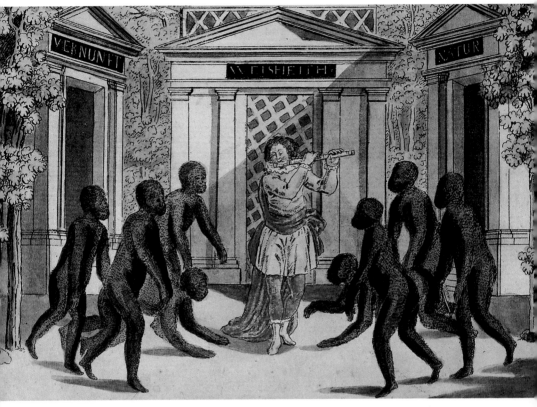

This drawing illustrates a scene from *The Magic Flute*. The fairy-tale opera was very popular with the working classes.

Back in Vienna the strange visitor returned to check on the progress of his funeral music. Mozart was frightened by the tall, thin man, whose ghostly presence was mysteriously cloaked in gray. Still sick, tired, and emotionally drained, Mozart had the eerie feeling that he was being asked to write the music for his own funeral.

The Last Season

On September 30, 1791, *The Magic Flute* opened with Mozart conducting. The story featured common people who became educated with wisdom, goodness, and love. The fairy-tale opera, with witches, monsters, and dazzling scenery, was very popular with Mozart's new suburban audience of working-class people.

As autumn turned to winter, Mozart became very ill while working on the requiem mass. He thought he had been poisoned, and he could not stop thinking that he was writing the music for his own funeral.

Papageno, the hero of *The Magic Flute,* plays his pipes. Mozart was pleased with the success of his final opera.

Mozart wrote his final composition, a funeral mass, as he lay dying. After Mozart's death, another composer completed the work.

As he lay on his sickbed, Mozart cherished the moments of happiness that came from news of the successes of *The Magic Flute*. For a while his health seemed to improve. Then, as he lay sick on December 4, Mozart told his wife and family that he was going to die that night. As his body became paralyzed, he said goodbye to his family. He also gave instructions on how the requiem should be finished. He died just after midnight on December 5, 1791. He was only thirty-five years old.

Passion and Sympathy

In the years after her husband died, Constanze worked very hard to get his music published and performed. The publishers of his music used the Latin version of his middle name, and he became known as Wolfgang Amadeus Mozart, one of the greatest musical geniuses that ever lived. Inspired by his attitude, many musicians that followed Mozart, such as Ludwig van Beethoven, refused to be treated as servants. Though the humanity and power of Mozart's music was not widely appreciated until many years after his death, his deep passion and sympathy changed musical expression forever.

Notes

Chapter 1: The Child Wonder

1. Quoted in Eric Schenk, *Mozart and His Times.* New York: Knopf, 1959, p. 42.

Chapter 2: The Young Composer

2. Quoted in Schenk, *Mozart and His Times,* p. 158.

Chapter 3: Seeking Success and Happiness

3. Quoted in Schenk, *Mozart and His Times,* p. 238.

4. Quoted in Harold C. Schonberg, *The Lives of the Great Composers.* New York: W.W. Norton, 1981, p. 100.

Chapter 4: Operas and Funeral Music

5. Quoted in Michael Kelly, *Reminiscences,* vol. 1. New York: Oxford University Press, 1975, pp. 258–59.

6. Quoted in Nathan Broder, *The Great Operas of Mozart.* New York: W.W. Norton, 1962, p. 68.

7. Quoted in E.S. Tchernaya, *Mozart His Life and Times.* Neptune City, NJ: THF, 1986, p. 156.

Glossary

archbishop: A Christian cleric of the highest rank having the right and power to interpret and apply the law in his territory.

composer: One who creates a piece of music.

concerto: Music written for one or more instrumental soloists and an orchestra.

conductor: One who directs an orchestra or other such group.

director: A person who supervises the creative aspects of a dramatic production and instructs the actors and crew.

libretto: The story of an opera, written by an author called a librettist, that a composer puts to music.

opera: A musical comedy or drama that is totally or mostly sung.

prodigy: A person, usually a child, with exception talents or powers.

string quartet: A musical group that includes two violins, a viola, and a cello. The term also refers to a composition written for these four instruments.

symphony: A long piece of music in three or more movements for symphony orchestra, basically a large-scale sonata with interwoven parts.

For Further Exploration

Catherine Brighton, *Mozart: Scenes from the Childhood of the Great Composer.* New York: Doubleday, 1990. A storybook tale of people, places, and events in the lives of Wolfgang and Nannerl Mozart.

Francene Sabin, *Mozart, Young Music Genius.* Mahwa, NJ: Troll, 1990. A biography of Mozart, emphasizing the first six years of his life.

Wendy Thompson, *Composer's World: Wolfgang Amadeus Mozart.* New York: Viking Penguin, 1990. This book tells how Mozart's life and work is related to the time and place he lived in.

Mike Venezia, *Getting to Know the World's Greatest Composers: Wolfgang Amadeus Mozart.* Chicago: Childrens Press, 1995. A biography of the child prodigy who wrote more than eight hundred pieces of music before he died at the age of thirty-five.

Roland Vernon, *Introducing Mozart.* Parsippany, NJ: Silver Burdett, 1996. The story of the composer's life, including his fame as a childhood prodigy, his musical career, and his early death in 1791.

Index

Abduction from the Harem, The, 29

Ascanio in Alba, 17

Bavaria, elector of, 19

characteristics
  insecurity, 21
  poor treatment of others, 24
  pride, 12
Charlotte (queen of
  England), 12
Clemency of Titus, The, 36
Colloredo, Hieronymus von,
  18–19, 22, 26–28
compositions
  disappearance of, 24
  first, 10
  religious, 17, 18, 36, 38,
    39
  types of, 21–22
  see also specific titles of
    operas
concertos, 10, 21–22

da Ponte, Lorenzo, 32–33,
  35–36
diseases, 13, 15
Don Giovanni, 33

George III (king of
  England), 12

Haydn, Joseph, 19

Idomeneo, King of Crete, 27
Italy, 15–17

Kelly, Michael, 33

Leopold II (emperor of
  Austria), 36
lifestyle, 34–35
London (England), 12

Magic Flute, The, 36, 38–39
Maria Theresa (empress of
  Holy Roman Empire), 11
Marie Antoinette (daughter
  of Maria Theresa), 11
Marriage of Figaro, The,
  32–33
Mithridate, King of Pontus,
  16–17
Mozart, Anna Maria
  (mother), 6, 23, 25
Mozart, Carl Thomas (son),
  31
Mozart, Constanze Weber
  (wife), 29, 30, 41
Mozart, Franz Xavier (son),
  36
Mozart, Leopold (father)
  birth of Wolfgang and, 6
  Constanze and, 29, 30
  control of Wolfgang by, 23
  illness of, 12
  as musician, 6, 8
Mozart, Maria Anna

Walburga Ignatia (sister)
See Mozart, Nannerl (sister)
Mozart, Nannerl (sister)
  Constanze and, 30
  health of, 13, 15
  as musician, 9
Mozart, Wolfgang Amadeus
  appearance of, 15, 18
  birth of, 6
  children of, 31, 35, 36
  as concert director, 18
  as court organist, 18, 26
  death of, 41
  health of, 13, 15, 31, 39, 41
  marriage of, 29
  musical ability of, 8–9
  nicknames of, 6, 7, 41
  performances by, as child,
    11–12, 14
  performances by, as
    teenager, 17–18
musicians as servants, 11–12

names, 7, 41

operas. *See specific titles*

Paris, 24–25
patrons, 11–12, 29
perfect pitch, 8–9, 11
Prague (Czech Republic),
  33
Prague (symphony), 33
Pretend Gardener Girl, The,
  19–20
Pretend Idiot, The, 15

requiem mass, 36, 38, 39

Salzburg (Austria), 6, 18,
  26
Schikaneder, Emanuel, 36
smallpox, 15
sound, sensitivity to, 9, 24
string quartets, 17
symphonies, 13, 17, 33

They're All the Same, 35–36

Vienna (Austria), 28–29,
  30–31

Weber family, 28–29

Picture Credits

Cover Image: Iconographico S.A./CORBIS

© Alinari/Art Resource, NY, 16, 34 (timeline)

© Austrian Archives/CORBIS, 39

© Corel Corporation, 18, 34 (timeline)

© Iconographico S.A./CORBIS, 35 (timeline)

Chris Jouan, 9, 34-35

© Erich Lessing/Art Resource, NY, 7, 10, 14, 20, 25, 26, 28, 34 (timeline), 37, 38

Library of Congress, 40

© Mary Evans Picture Library, 30, 35 (timeline)

© Gianni Dagli Orti/CORBIS, 23

© Scala/Art Resource, NY, 18, 21, 35 (timeline)

© Victoria & Albert Museum, London/Art Resource, NY, 13

About the Authors

P.M. Boekhoff is an author of more than twenty-five nonfiction books for children. She has written about history, science, and the lives of creative people. In addition Boekhoff is an artist who has created murals and theatrical scenics and illustrated many book covers. In her spare time she paints, draws, writes poetry, and studies herbal medicine.

Stuart A. Kallen is the author of more than 150 nonfiction books for children and young adults. He has written extensively about Native Americans and American history. In addition, Kallen has written award-winning children's videos and television scripts. In his spare time he is a singer/songwriter/guitarist in San Diego, California.